Do current legal regimes encourage or prevent consumers from extracting various benefits from electronic commerce? A growing literature examines how electronic commerce affects the prices and availability of numerous physical goods. Economic theory provides reasons that online prices could be either higher or lower than offline prices, with empirical scholarship reporting mixed results. Online commerce also may increase the variety of products available to consumers, because the products that are not available in bricks-and-mortar stores that are within a reasonable distance or with reasonable search costs may be available online. As with prices, however, the size of the variety effect is an empirical question.

Even if consumers can benefit from cost savings and/or greater variety by shopping online, the current regulatory and legal landscape that governs electronic commerce may affect the degree to which consumers can realize these benefits. This paper tries to assess the manner in which the current legal framework governing wine and alcohol distribution and sales might affect electronic commerce in wine. We provide a modest empirical examination of the potential cost savings and product selection that might be available online to consumers in a particular state in the absence of certain legal restrictions.

The paper is organized as follows. Section 1 provides a brief discussion of the existing literature and commentary on potential cost savings of electronic commerce as well as the policy implications of Internet wine sales. Section 2 discusses, in more detail, the current legal framework that governs interstate alcohol sales and outlines theoretical expectations about what (if any) differences should exist between online and offline wine prices and product inventories. Section 3 discusses the data collection methods employed for our price and product variety comparison between online and offline retail channels, and Section 4 presents the findings. Section 5 concludes with a summary, some caveats, and a brief discussion of prospects for future research.

Section 1: Literature and Policy Issues

This study adds to the quickly growing body of scholarship that investigates whether consumers can realize nontrivial benefits by shopping online rather than, or in addition to, bricks-and-mortar outlets. Considering the body of existing research, empirical findings are mixed. In auto retailing, for example, users of a referral site that facilitates price competition among dealers (autobytel.com) pay lower prices than they otherwise would have paid (Scott Morton, Zettlemeyer, and Silva-Risso 2001; Zettlemeyer, Scott Morton, and Silva-Risso 2001). Some studies of online auto auctions, CDs, books, and software, in contrast, have found that prices are higher online (Lee 1997, Bailey 1998a, b). A more recent study of books and CDs found that online prices are lower (Brynjolfsson and Smith 2000). Besides price savings, the present study also addresses questions about product variety that consumers may encounter online. Whether these benefits are significant or trivial is an empirical matter, and little scholarship has focused on this particular question.

Studies of prices and product availability in electronic markets are highly relevant to public policy, because many types of regulations may inhibit consumers' ability to purchase specific products online. A recent Federal Trade Commission workshop revealed a wide variety of restrictions affecting the online availability of products as diverse as contact lenses, automobiles, books, real estate, caskets, pharmaceuticals, wine,

2

and virtually all types of secondhand merchandise.[2] A better understanding of the costs and benefits of these regulations to consumers could lead to a more informed policy debate.

Along these lines, perhaps no e-commerce topic generates as much controversy as online wine sales. In this debate traditional consumer concerns, such as price and variety, are commonly balanced against other significant public policy goals. In many states, laws prevent or hamper online wine sales by prohibiting out-of-state retailers or wineries from shipping wine directly to customers. Proponents of these laws argue that the economic harm to consumers is slight, and that these laws are necessary to promote temperance, collect alcohol taxes, and prevent underage drinking. (Gray 2002, Hurd 2002, Mead 2002, Painter 2002) Opponents claim that consumers suffer significant harm, and that legitimate concerns about taxation and alcoholic beverage control can be addressed through policies that are less restrictive than an outright ban on direct shipment. (Genesen 2002, Gross 2002, McFadden 2002, Sloane 2002)

Despite a wide array of arguments on both sides, no substantial data (or analysis) has been offered that would allow policymakers to assess the impact of alternative policies on consumers. We seek to remedy part of this gap by comparing online and offline wine prices and product variety for a political jurisdiction where direct shipment from out-of-state wine sellers is prohibited: McLean, Virginia. At the time the data for this study were gathered, the Commonwealth of Virginia banned direct shipment of

---

[2] See http://www.ftc.gov/opp/ecommerce/anticompetitive/index.htm.

alcoholic beverages to Virginia residents by out-of-state vendors, but permitted direct shipment by in-state wineries, breweries, and retailers.[3]

Drawing on price data from online wine retailers, wineries that sell online, and bricks-and-mortar wine retailers in Northern Virginia, this study offers a snapshot of the retail landscape that a consumer in McLean, Virginia faces when seeking to purchase relatively popular wines in the presence of a ban on direct shipment by out-of-state sellers. By foreclosing online wine purchases from out-of-state sellers, Virginia's direct shipment ban reduces the product selection available to consumers and prevents consumers from purchasing many premium wines at lower prices online.

Section 2: Legal Regimes and Potential Impacts

Alcohol Regulation

Unlike most consumer goods that are shipped across state lines, interstate alcohol sales operate under an extremely stringent legal framework. States commonly employ a "three-tiered" system in which manufacturing (i.e., distilling, fermenting, or brewing), wholesaling, and retailing are vertically dis-integrated.[4] The Virginia statute offers a typical justification for the ban on vertical integration:

> The General Assembly finds that it is necessary and proper to require a
> separation between manufacturing interests, wholesale interests and retail
> interests in the production and distribution of alcoholic beverages in order
> to prevent suppliers from dominating local markets through vertical

---

[3] In March 2002, a federal court declared this law unconstitutional under the Commerce Clause in the belief that it discriminates against out-of-state sellers. Directly following the ruling, the court granted a stay in order to give the state legislature an opportunity to correct provisions of the law found to be unconstitutional. *Bolick v. Roberts*, 199 F. Supp. 2d 397 (E.D. Va. 2002). In the 2003 legislative session, the Virginia General Assembly overwhelmingly approved legislation that would permit out-of-state firms to ship beer and wine to consumers in Virginia if they obtain a permit and remit relevant taxes. This legislation awaits the Governor's signature at the time this study was released. Direct shipment from out-of-state was thus illegal at the time the data for this study were gathered.

[4] The principal exception occurs when states that sell distilled spirits through state-owned liquor stores also choose to perform the wholesaling function, receiving shipments direct from distillers.

integration and to prevent excessive sales of alcoholic beverages caused by overly aggressive marketing techniques. (VA Code Sec. 4.1-215.C)

Most wine purchased by Virginia consumers passes through the three-tier system, although in-state wineries are allowed to sell direct to Virginia consumers. Out-of-state wineries must sell to a firm that possesses a license to import wine into Virginia. The importer must then sell to a Virginia wholesaler, who supplies retailers. Wholesalers often also hold licenses to import, and because out-of-state firms cannot obtain Virginia wholesale or retail licenses, their wines must pass through these Virginia businesses before they reach customers (VA Code Sec. 4.1-207).

The direct shipment ban is hardly unique to Virginia. As of July 2002 (when the data for this study were gathered), 23 states allowed interstate direct shipments of wine under certain conditions, whereas 27 prohibited it, with seven states classifying direct wine shipments as a felony.[5] While 27 states prohibited interstate direct sales, only 20 states prohibited intrastate direct sales.[6] In seven states, including Virginia, an in-state

---

[5] Of those states that allow interstate direct sales, 13 are classified as "reciprocity" states. These states recognize two-way shipping rights between jurisdictions. Just because a state is reciprocal does not necessarily mean that it permits interstate wine shipments from all states. Rather, reciprocity only guarantees that shipping rights from other reciprocal states are acknowledged. In addition, the shipping rights might be restricted only to other reciprocal states. Similarly, the shipping rights might also depend on the kind of wines being shipped, relative alcohol contents, etc. Besides the states that are reciprocal, ten states allow limited direct wine shipments through personal importation laws that allow consumers to receive wine from another state, subject to certain conditions. In some states this privilege requires written approval from the relevant authorities, involves a very limited amount of alcohol, or is subject to other specific state-by-state restrictions.

While unknown to many consumers, personal importation or transportation laws in several states expressly prohibit bringing alcohol across state lines without going through the appropriate distribution channels. Hence, if a consumer drives cross country with a case of wine in his car, he may unwittingly violate a myriad of state-level alcohol laws during his journey as he enters and exits states. Virginia permits individuals to bring into the state, in their personal possession, one gallon or four liters of alcoholic beverages "not for resale," and new residents can bring in a "reasonable quantity" of alcoholic beverages "not for resale" as part of their household goods. (VA Code Sec. 4.1-310.E) In response to post-9/11 restrictions that have made it more difficult for travelers to bring wine home on airplanes, a new federal law permits individuals who place an order in person at a winery to ship to their residences the same amount of wine that their state law would permit them to physically carry into the state.

[6] Several states that ban direct shipment from out-of-state but permit direct shipment from in-state wineries or retailers have seen their bans challenged as unconstitutional restrictions on interstate commerce. Two

winery can ship wine directly to an in-state customer, but that same customer cannot legally have wine shipped to his residence from another state.[7] Appendix A provides a state-by-state breakdown of direct wine sales laws as of July 2002.

Online Prices and Variety: Hypotheses

Laws that permit direct shipment of wine allow wineries and other merchants to compete with in-state bricks-and-mortar retailers who are supplied by wholesalers under the three-tier system. Direct shipment facilitates Internet wine sales by making it possible for these competitors to send their products directly to consumers instead of through the three-tier system of the state in which the customer lives. Both proponents and opponents seem to regard legal direct shipment as a necessary condition for e-commerce in wine.

Therefore, legalized direct shipping offers consumers access to hundreds of wineries and retailers across the nation, rather than the limited number that a typical consumer would likely seek out and visit in the course of shopping offline. Even if a local bricks-and-mortar retail wine market is highly competitive and includes retailers

---

such state bans have been upheld in legal challenges, three have been overturned, and two are pending. *Bainbridge v. Bush*, 148 F. Supp. 2d 1306 (M.D. Fl. 2001), *vacated on other grounds, Bainbridge v. Turner*, 311 F.3d 1104 (11th Cir. 2002)(Florida), *Heald v. Engler*, No. 00-CV-71438-DT, slip op. (E.D. Mich. Sept. 28, 2001)(Michigan), *Bolick v. Roberts*, 199 F. Supp. 2d 397 (E.D. Va. 2002)(Virginia), *Beskind v. Easley*, 197 F. Supp. 2d 464 (W.D.N.C. 2002)(North Carolina), *Dickerson v. Bailey*, 212 F. Supp. 2d 673 (S.D. Tex. 2002), *incorporating Dickerson v. Bailey* 87 F.Supp.2d 691 (S.D. Tex. 2000)(Texas), *Swedenburg v. Kelly*, 232 F. Supp. 2d 135 (S.D.N.Y. 2002)(New York), *Mast v. Long*, No. CS-01-00298, 2002 WL 31039421, slip op. (E.D. Wash. Sept. 9, 2002)(Washington).

[7] Our discussions with several wine retailers outside of Virginia reveal that some wine retailers and wineries will ship directly into Virginia, while others will not. When the shipping retailers were asked how this activity was legal under Virginia law, they said that when they sell the wine to the consumer and then arrange shipment via 3rd-party carrier, they are effectively transferring ownership of the wine to the consumer and then helping him "ship it to himself." From a legal standpoint then, these retailers claimed that they were absolving themselves of all legal liability once the consumer purchased the wine, and it was the consumer's responsibility to determine whether state law permits such shipments. According to the winery/retailer, it is in compliance with the law, even if the Virginia consumer is unwittingly breaking the law by shipping wine across state lines to himself. For the purposes of this study, we presume that Virginia's direct shipment ban is a binding constraint – an assumption consistent with the existence of

offering large inventories, we would expect that a consumer could find some additional varieties and better prices when given the option of searching several hundred retailers nationwide.

Nevertheless, economic theory provides several, often conflicting, expectations regarding whether online prices may be higher or lower than offline prices, and whether online shopping gives consumers access to varieties of products that are not available offline within a reasonable distance of the customer. The following section provides a brief discussion of these different perspectives.

Potential price effects

Why online prices may be lower

There are four possible reasons why online wine prices generally might be lower than offline wine prices: many more sellers, lower search costs, less market power, and lower cost of the online sales channel. (Smith, Bailey, and Brynjolfsson 1999).

The first, and most obvious, explanation for why consumers are sometimes likely to find lower prices by searching online is that the number of online sellers greatly exceeds the number of local retail sellers – particularly the number of local retail sellers whose inventories a consumer could check with reasonable search costs. The online shopbot we used to gather wine prices, Winesearcher.com, can access more than 700 online retailers and a number of wineries – many more than a consumer likely would visit in person. Even if average prices were the same online and offline, the opportunity to search many more retailers online means that the consumer is more likely to encounter a lower price online.

---

high-profile litigation, court findings in that litigation, and the push to remove the ban in the 2003 legislative session.

Another explanation for why online prices may be lower than offline prices is based on search costs. By reducing the cost of searching price and nonprice attributes, e-commerce could lead to low retail margins and prices online. (Bakos 1997, 2001:71; Wiseman 2001: 28-29) Previous empirical research in other industries has found that online purchases are highly elastic with respect to both online and offline prices (Goolsbee 2001, 2000; Ellison and Ellison 2001; Goolsbee and Chevalier 2002).[8] If wine consumers are price-sensitive, then price-cutting could be a viable business strategy for an electronic wine retailer.

A third economic explanation for why online wine sellers might charge lower prices is that they may be able to circumvent the wholesaler markup paid by offline retailers without incurring substantial alternative costs. Critics of the three-tier system often argue that it may create inefficiencies or create market power for wholesalers by creating barriers to entry (state licensing) and limiting intrabrand competition by requiring producers to give exclusive territories to wholesalers. (Gross 2002:3; Sloane 2002:2) Staff of federal antitrust agencies has often opposed state efforts to strengthen the three-tier system on similar grounds.[9]

In the case of Virginia, for example, licensing may create barriers to entry in several ways. One type of entrant -- the out-of-state business -- simply cannot obtain a Virginia wine wholesaler's license. In addition, the Alcoholic Beverage Control Board

---

[8] Contrary to this research, Degeratu, Rangaswamy, and Wu (1998) found that online grocery purchasers are less price sensitive than offline grocery purchasers
[9] See, e.g., comments of Federal Trade Commission Staff on proposals in Illinois, North Carolina, and Massachusetts at http://www.ftc.gov/be/v990005.htm http://www.ftc.gov/be/v990003.htm and http://www.ftc.gov/be/v960012.htm.

may decline to grant any type of alcohol license for a variety of reasons, including one that appears to grant substantial discretion; a license can be denied if:

> The number of licenses existent in the locality is such that the granting of a license is detrimental to the interest, morals, safety or welfare of the public. (VA Code Sec. 4.1-222 A.3)

Most available empirical studies find that laws permitting or requiring territorial exclusivity for wholesalers of alcoholic beverages do indeed raise prices. (See, e.g., Jordan and Jaffee 1987, Culbertson and Bradford 1991, Sass and Saurman 1996.) While Virginia law bans exclusive territories, it requires the winery to designate a "primary area of responsibility" for each wholesaler to whom it sells, and the winery can have only one distributor in each territory for a single established brand (Code of Virginia Sec. 4.1-404.). Primary areas of responsibility may have the same effect as exclusive territories if wholesalers generally refrain from selling to retailers outside of their primary area of responsibility.

Some aspects of Virginia's three-tier system might confer market power on wholesalers. Direct shipping allows wineries to circumvent this market power by selling direct to consumers online. In addition, to the extent that online customers purchase wine from retailers rather than wineries, direct shipping could reduce market power by placing retailers and wholesalers in different geographic markets in competition with each other. Online wine prices could thus be lower because they might reflect the more competitive conditions online, whereas offline prices could be higher than online prices if local wholesalers possess market power.

Finally, Internet wine prices may be lower if Internet vendors possess lower cost structures or other efficiency advantages. An Internet retailer or winery may have a fundamentally different business model that incurs less of the traditional retail costs (stores, sales personnel, etc.)[10] A winery that sells direct to consumers can also bypass transaction cost inefficiencies created by state alcohol franchise laws, which often make it prohibitively costly for a winery to switch wholesalers.

Considering Virginia again, state law specifies that a winery cannot terminate its agreement with a wholesaler in the absence of "good cause," such as state revocation of the wholesaler's license, bankruptcy of the wholesaler, failure to maintain a sales volume or trend for the brand comparable to that of other Virginia wholesalers that carry the brand, or other factors. The wholesaler must be given 60 days to cure any deficiency, and the state's Department of Alcoholic Beverage Control ultimately determines good cause after a hearing. (VA Code Sec. 4.1-406) Virginia law also requires wholesalers to pay an annual licensing fee of $715-$1,430, depending on volume; local governments are permitted to charge an additional $50 license tax. Wholesalers must also post a surety bond of $100,000. (VA Code Sec. 4.1-223.4) Finally, a wholesaler who wants to import must obtain a wine importer's license that costs $285 annually. (VA Code Sec. 4.1-231.2) To the extent that such restrictions increase risk, increase costs, and reduce distribution flexibility, Internet wine retailers may have a cost advantage if they can obtain wine from wholesalers in states with less burdensome regulations. Alternatively, the winery can avoid the regulatory costs created by wine wholesale franchise laws by

---

[10] One possibility is that online retailers possess lower costs because they can "free ride" off of pre-sale services, such as wine tastings or wine appreciation classes, provided by bricks-and-mortar retailers. To our knowledge, no scholarship has examined the possibility of free-riding in the context of online wine sales. Interestingly, no parties testifying on the (highly contentious) wine panel at the FTC's October 2002 workshop on barriers to e-commerce raised the free rider issue, although it was discussed on panels dealing other industries, such as automobiles. See http://www.ftc.gov/opp/ecommerce/anticompetitive/agenda.htm

selling direct via the Internet. In either case, the retail price of wine on the Internet could be lower.

Online wine prices might also be lower due to direct sales from wineries that enjoy transaction cost efficiencies as a result of vertical integration. Two economics papers (Gertner 1999, Gertner and Stillman 2001) suggest that vertically integrated retailers are more likely to sell direct online because vertical integration can lower coordination costs, help solve externality problems, and mitigate channel conflict. Empirical evidence from retailing is consistent with the hypothesis that manufacturers who are already integrated into retailing initiate direct online sales more quickly than non-integrated apparel producers. If vertical integration produces transaction cost efficiencies for wineries, it is also plausible that some of those efficiencies may be passed through to consumers in the form of lower prices. Wineries selling direct may charge lower prices than bricks-and-mortar retailers, and other online merchants may even feel compelled to match these prices.[11]

Why online prices may be higher

The literature on e-commerce offers two hypotheses suggesting why online wine prices could be higher than offline prices: value of consumers' time, and reduced search costs for quality attributes.

If Internet wine sellers are not the lowest-cost suppliers, they may charge a higher price and survive because their customers find the convenience worth the extra cost. In

---

[11] In Virginia, direct shipment provides the only avenue by which out-of-state wineries could integrate forward into retailing, because all out-of-state wine sold in bricks-and-mortar stores must first pass through independent wholesalers. Indeed, one of the explicitly stated purposes of Virginia's Alcoholic Beverage Control laws is to prevent vertical integration. (The only exception is for in-state wineries, which can make retail sales to customers who visit the winery and can ship directly to customers in Virginia.)

their discussion of price dispersion, Smith, Bailey, and Brynjolffson (1999: 109) suggest that e-retailers who "make it easier to find and evaluate products may be able to charge a price premium to time-sensitive customers." A similar theory could be advanced to explain why Internet prices could exceed offline prices for identical products. Assume that a subset of consumers have a high value of time and thus incur high search costs if they attempt to compare prices at bricks and mortar stores. These customers would likely be willing to pay a premium for the privilege of not having to search multiple physical stores – and not even having to travel to a single store -- to get their wine. Customers with low search and travel costs might still check the Internet prices as part of their search, but they would likely patronize the lower-priced bricks-and-mortar stores.

Perceived product differentiation presents an alternative reason that online wine sales could be higher than offline prices. By reducing the cost of obtaining information on quality attributes, online sales could increase customers' ability to perceive differences between different varieties of wine. As customers are better able to select wines that match their individual tastes, they become less price-sensitive. Experimental evidence is consistent with this theory (Lynch and Ariely 2000). If online wine buyers make greater use of such information than offline buyers, then online buyers may be less price-sensitive and online prices could be higher.

For either of these theories to work, there must be some impediment that prevents online retailers from competing away their profit margins by offering lower prices to consumers or paying higher prices for their wine supplies. For this reason, these theories may more accurately describe how online pricing works when an electronic market is in its infancy and there are few competitors, or when some other barrier prevents the emergence of significant online competition.

Potential variety effects

Why online variety may be greater

There are three principal reasons that consumers may have access to a greater variety of wines online: larger numbers of retailers, intentional product differentiation, and lower fixed costs of marketing and distribution.

The number of online retailers whose products a consumer could search greatly exceeds the number of local retailers that a consumer could reasonably search. One would expect that access to a substantially larger number of retailers would expand the variety of products from which a consumer could choose.

An economic theory that would predict greater product variety online is based on product differentiation. Electronic commerce can facilitate price competition for products that are close substitutes, thus eroding retail margins (Ellison and Ellison 2001). Product differentiation is a possible strategy for muting price competition (Bakos 1997; 2001:71-72; Lynch and Ariely 2000; Wiseman 2000: 30). For online wine sales, differentiation could take several forms that would increase the available number of labels. For example, online merchants could seek out more obscure labels that were not previously available through bricks-and-mortar stores, or lesser-known labels could become available if wineries found that consumers attach greater cachet to wines ordered direct from the winery.[12]

---

[12] One far-fetched possibility is that wineries could proliferate the number of labels by developing different blends of grape varieties (and adding other fruit juices for non-purists). Over the long run, vineyards may develop and cultivate a larger number of new varieties of grapes, and additional small wineries with distinctive characteristics may come into existence. Given the early state of online commerce and the

Even if wineries and e-retailers do not consciously seek to increase differentiation in order to reduce price competition, online wine sales could increase variety simply due to the relative costs of selling wine online vs. through bricks-and-mortar stores. Advocates of direct shipping frequently assert that online wine sales give consumers access to a greater variety of wines than they can obtain by visiting the local retailer (Genesen 2002, Gross 2002, McFadden 2002, Sloane 2002). Even with the best distribution system possible, there are several products that wine producers simply will not sell through channels beyond their tasting rooms (or by other direct means). If a consumer who lives in a state that bans interstate direct wine shipments finds himself in a Napa Valley tasting room, he may find a product that he would like to acquire at home. Yet, he may not be able to obtain the wine from a local retailer because the winery does not sell through a wholesale distributor.

The economic theory implicit in this example is that selling a wine through offline retail stores may entail fixed costs (for the vineyard, wholesaler, and/or retailer) that are prohibitively high for relatively small quantities of a particular wine (McFadden 2002:1). Internet technology dramatically lowers the fixed cost of making consumers aware that a particular product or variety even exists (Bakos 2001: 71). Online sales may thus have lower fixed costs per winery, brand, or variety. While the variable costs (e.g. shipping) may be higher, the fixed costs may be sufficiently lower that wineries may profit from online distribution even if sale through the three-tier system is unprofitable. Under these conditions, online shopping should provide access to greater variety.

---

substantial lead times involved in developing new wineries and grape varieties, we expect that online commerce has had little effect on these latter factors to date.

Why online variety may be no greater

An alternative product variety hypothesis is offered by wine wholesalers and alcoholic beverage regulators: any product for which there is customer demand can make its way into the existing distribution system. As evidence they cite public opinion polls revealing that the vast majority of alcohol drinkers are satisfied with the selection of beer and wine available in from local retailers (Gray 2002: 4), and relatively little utilization by wineries of legal direct shipping laws enacted by some states (Painter 2002). In economic terms, the se parties are suggesting that fixed costs of getting a particular label into the three-tier system are not high enough to reduce variety to any meaningful extent; therefore, if a winery cannot find wholesalers to carry its wines, consumer demand must be negligible.

Section 3: Data Sources and Calculations

There is little empirical information on how access to out-of-state wine sellers through the Internet affects the prices and varieties of wines available to consumers. To address this void, this study analyzes the prices and wine selections offered by stores that identify themselves as wine retailers in the greater McLean, Virginia, area for a pre-identified market bundle of popular wines. McLean was chosen as the relevant retail area for several reasons. First, Virginia bars direct sales, and hence it is an appropriate state for which to consider the effects of direct sales laws on product selection and price. Second, given the socio-economic status of many residents in McLean (and Northern Virginia, generally), it seemed likely that several bricks-and-mortar outlets could be found locally that catered to the needs of a sophisticated wine drinking population. As a result, any estimate of the "variety effect" would likely be conservative and could not be dismissed as driven by the choice of a location where few fine wines would likely be available.[13] Due to the choice of locality, our results should be interpreted as a comparison of the online and offline prices and product variety available in a locality likely to have a high demand for "better" wines, rather than an illustration of prices and variety available to a "typical" consumer.

The wine sample

In an effort to select an unbiased sample of wines that are likely to be popular among wine drinkers who are likely to frequent wine stores, the wine data for this study was drawn from the 13th Annual Restaurant Poll conducted by *Wine and Spirits* magazine. The findings from this poll were published in their April 2002 issue, which identified the "Top 50 Wines" overall, as well as by varietal. One of the benefits of using the *Wine and Spirits* list, rather than a list compiled by a different publication, is that *Wine and Spirits* actually relies on consumer demand for individual wines in compiling their rankings, rather than "expert" opinions, which may be unrepresentative of the wine-drinking public. More specifically, to determine the "Top 50," the publishers sent out a questionnaire on wine sales to 1,995 restaurants in the United States; 381 restaurants responded. The survey asked (among other questions) what each restaurant's top ten selling wines were in the last quarter of 2001. For each of the ten wines listed on a restaurant's response, *Wine and Spirits* assigned a point value ranging from ten (for the best selling wine) to one (for the tenth best selling wine), which contributed towards its

---

[13] While McLean was chosen, any community in Northern Virginia that was reasonably close to Washington, DC, would be equally appropriate for this study. Given the nature of the data being considered, it is doubtful that the results presented below would differ appreciably if the market being studied was somewhere other than McLean (with the possible exception that the more-expensive wines might be more difficult to find in less affluent areas).

list of the most popular wines (which were arranged by varietal). For example, if Winery X held spots 1-3 on Restaurant Y's wine list for its Chardonnay, Cabernet Sauvignon, and Merlot, respectively, then its Chardonnay would receive 10 points, its Cabernet would receive 9 points, and its Merlot would receive 8 points, respectively. The ranking of each wine was determined, then, by summing the scores across all respondents.[14]

Given the list of most popular wines, arranged by varietal, the 50 highest point recipients were selected for price comparisons from the collection of Sauvignon Blancs, Chardonnays, Cabernet Sauvignons, Merlots, Pinot Noirs, and Zinfandels produced by American winemakers. The highest ranked wine in this sample is the Sonoma-Cutrer Vineyards Chardonnay, with 464 points, while the 50th-most popular wine is a five-way tie between Caymus Vineyards' and Kendall Jackson Vineyards' Cabernet Sauvignon, Rodney Strong Vineyards' Merlot, La Crema's Pinot Noir, and Murphy-Goode's Sauvignon Blanc with 41 points each. The complete sample of wines analyzed is listed in Appendix B. As can be seen, focusing our attention on the top 50 point recipients actually identifies 83 individual bottles. The difference between ordinal rankings (the Top 50) and sample size (83) follows from the fact that *Wine and Sprits* recognizes all relevant bottles that fall under a given wineries' varietal when it identifies the most popular Chardonnays, Merlots, etc. For example, Cakebread's chardonnay received 244 points, making it the third most popular wine overall, but Wine and Spirits recognized two bottles, the "Napa Valley" and the "Napa Valley Reserve," as "Cakebread Chardonnay," and hence both were included in our sample.

---

[14] Questions might be raised over whether this list truly represents the most popular wines in the United States, as some of the best selling wines overall (i.e., "jug" wines) are not in this list. While it may be true that certain best selling (and lower quality) wines are not represented in this sample, we find it unlikely that

Taking this list of 83 bottles, the relevant wineries were contacted, either by phone or Internet, to determine whether all bottlings were available for retail sale, as well as the year of the most recent vintage. Appendix B identifies four bottles with an asterisk that were either unavailable for retail sale to consumers (i.e., they were only sold to restaurants), had been misnamed by *Wine and Spirits*, or could otherwise not be found online. The remaining 79 bottles, which were identified as being currently available vintages, were used for price comparisons between offline and online retail channels.

Price and variety searches

We designed our study so that it would reasonably simulate how a serious wine consumer might shop. The online shopper, of course, can access hundreds of retailers and wineries; the shopbot we used to gather prices, "Winesearcher.com," had access to more than 700 wine stores with online inventory access and also listed wine price data from some wineries. We assumed that legalized direct shipping would permit the McLean consumer to order from any of these online sources.

For offline shopping, it is doubtful that a consumer would physically visit (or even phone) every possible source of wine in the area. Consulting "Yahoo! Yellow Pages," we collected a list of every store identifying itself as a "wine retailer" located within a ten-mile radius of McLean.[15] We assumed that a McLean consumer would search several nearby stores that carry large inventories at attractive prices. To guard against the possibility that even large retailers might not always carry a full array of

---

these wines would be among those that serious wine drinkers might consider for regular purchase/consumption.

[15] Because Virginia state law expressly bans the importation of alcohol from other states, we only focused our attention on those stores within the ten-mile radius that were located in Virginia. Several reviewers of this paper who drink wine and live in Northern Virginia doubted that a wine consumer would search all 13 wine retailers we identified. If they are correct, then our price and variety findings likely under-estimate the potential benefits of legalized direct shipping.

lesser-known wines that they could obtain from wholesalers, we also assumed that the consumer might check a number of smaller, specialty wine shops. The list that emerged consisted of the 13 retail outlets identified in Appendix C; it includes several "wine megastores" (Total Beverage) as well as smaller wine shops.

Our sample does not include general grocery stores (e.g., Giant, Safeway) or club stores (e.g., Costco). However, two of the bricks-and-mortar stores searched were beverage megastores known for carrying very large selections at competitive prices. In the personal shopping experience of the authors and several reviewers of this paper, these megastores' everyday prices tend to be lower than or equal to those of grocery stores, but the grocery stores often beat the megastores' prices on lower-priced wines advertised as weekly specials. Hence, if the exclusion of grocery stores affects our price data, it likely overstates the offline prices for some of the less expensive wines that may have been offered by a grocer at a special, lower price at some point during the period when we collected our data. To assess whether the absence of grocery stores affects our results on variety, we made followup visits to several large grocery stores in McLean to see if they carried any of the wines that were unavailable at the stores in our sample that were listed as wine retailers in the Yellow Pages. They did not.

The first step in collecting price information was to contact the wineries directly and find out what prices the wineries were charging for their bottles. It is obvious, however, that there may be other retail channels available through the Internet that might sell wine for prices lower than those available at wineries.

To collect price data from other Internet-based stores, we engaged Winesearcher.com to collect the lowest online retail prices for each bottle in our sample.

The store name where each bottle was found, as well as its zip code, was also collected and used in calculating transportation costs. Using the shopbot, prices could be found for each of the 79 bottles. Comparing the Winesearcher.com price and the prices collected directly from the wineries, the least expensive price for each bottle was identified as the "best online price" at the time of data collection.

After collecting price data from out-of-state vendors, our next step was to collect price data for our sample from bricks-and-mortar stores. Prices for the bottles in our sample were collected from the 13 bricks-and-mortar retail outlets in one of two ways. Where the retail outlet had an Internet presence that listed its inventory and respective prices, price data were collected online. While these prices were not checked against physical inventory through on-site visits, for the purposes of this study it was assumed that the prices are identical to those in the store.[16] Those stores that had an appropriate web presence are indicated with an asterisk in Appendix C. Alternatively, for the remaining 10 stores, price data was collected by actually visiting the stores in early July 2002 and checking inventory on the shelves and recording its prices. All price data (on and offline) were collected between early June and early July 2002.

A critic might argue that special "sale" pricing during the month over which data were gathered may have distorted our online vs. offline price comparisons. With a search of more than 700 online stores versus 13 offline stores, the probability of finding a wine available at a sale price online may be greater than the probability of finding the same wine at a sale price offline (if individual online and offline wine merchants offer sale

---

[16] This assumption has been employed in similar price-comparison studies (e.g., Bailey (1998)).

prices with the same frequency). Our findings thus may overstate price savings for the customer who is content to wait until a sought-after wine comes on sale in a bricks-and-mortar store. On the other hand, any portion of our results that may stem from the increased probability of finding a wine on sale online counts as a legitimate cost saving for the customer who is unwilling to "time the market" and wait until a desired wine comes on sale offline.

Taxes and transportation costs

Retail sales and excise tax differentials could affect our price comparisons. We opted to compare prices without sales taxes, in order to ascertain whether Virginians who comply with all state sales and use tax laws (and would therefore pay these taxes both on wine purchased from out-of-state and on wine purchased locally) can save money buying wine online. While it is possible that shoppers in Virginia would try to evade sales taxes if they were allowed to buy online from out-of-state vendors, Virginia's legislation to remove the direct shipment ban requires shippers to obtain a state permit and remit applicable taxes. Wine industry representatives state that they are more than willing to remit taxes to states that permit them to ship directly to consumers. (See FTC 2002: 229) Hence, in the results that follow, sales taxes are not considered; our cost comparisons assume no cost savings due to sales tax evasion.

Excise taxes may also create price differentials if there are significant differences across states or if other states decline to charge excise taxes on wine exported to Virginia. Virginia's excise tax on wine is 40 cents/liter.[17] We declined to include the Virginia excise tax after discovering that a tax that small does not significantly change the results.

---

[17] Virginia Code Sec. 4.1-234.

Some of the online prices may include excise taxes imposed by other states, depending on the particular policy of the state where the wine exporter is located.[18]

To address transportation (i.e., shipping and handling) costs, the following procedure was used. For each bottle that would be purchased online, data were collected from the United Parcel Service website (www.ups.com) on the costs associated with shipping boxes of the appropriate size and weight to represent a single bottle, a half case, and a case of wine from the zip code where the online vendor was located (using a daily pickup service) into McLean, Virginia, under a variety of shipping options.[19] We estimated the cost of shipping larger quantities than a single bottle because an online shopper likely would purchase several bottles or an entire case of a given vintage. There are large economies of scale in shipping. Hence, the per-bottle shipping fee associated with an entire case, or at least multiple bottles, of each selection in the "Top 50" is significantly less than for an individual bottle.[20]

This method may either over- or under-state transportation costs to ship wine into McLean, for several reasons. First, because our search process found the least expensive bottle, and we then calculated the cost of shipping it to McLean, it is possible that we overlooked less expensive bottle price/shipping price combinations. For example, if a slightly more expensive bottle was identified, but it was closer to McLean, so it was much less expensive to ship than a bottle from a more distant location, our selection method would not identify this bottle for analysis. Second, this method ignores the

---

[18] California, for example, rebates excise taxes on all wine that is exported from the state.

[19] The weight and box dimension specifications were based on one of the authors' personal experience, in a political jurisdiction where direct shipping is legal, with out-of-state wine clubs that used packaging of these dimensions and weight for the bottles that they shipped.

[20] For example, it costs $8.81, $14.23, and $16.45 to ship one bottle from Palo Alto, CA to McLean, VA via standard ground, 3rd-day, and 2nd day shipping respectively. In contrast, if a consumer were ordering an

possibility that a single retailer might be the lowest-cost seller of more than one wine, and so even a customer who wanted only one or two bottles of a particular wine might reap economies of scale in shipping by ordering several different wines simultaneously from the same seller.

The calculation method also ignores the possibility that online wine retailers might impose handling charges in addition to the shipping costs. Since Virginia bans direct shipment, most of the online retailers do not quote shipping rates to McLean. In addition, most of the online retailers in our sample calculate shipping charges after the order is placed, so we do not have good information about additional handling charges or other markups on shipping charges for any delivery location. Several, however, do post shipping and handling information that is accessible without placing an order, and we checked the shipping and handling costs for ground delivery to Washington, DC, the jurisdiction closest to Northern Virginia that permits direct shipment (albeit limited). None of the online vendors who post such information imposes an additional handling charge. Some quote shipping charges that are higher than our estimate, which may indicate that a handling charge is bundled with the shipping charges as a markup. The typical shipping charge posted on web sites exceeds our single-bottle and six-bottle estimate by about $4-$5. Variances between posted and estimated 12-bottle shipping charges vary widely, from $16 below our estimate to $14 above, with a median of approximately $5. Unfortunately, we do not know whether these figures are typical for all online wine retailers in our sample, given that shipping cost data for the various quantities of wine were published on web sites by approximately six retailers. In

---

entire case from a retailer in Palo Alto, the per-bottle shipping charges would be $2.93, $5.40, and $6.98 for standard ground, 3rd-day, and 2nd-day shipping respectively.

addition, a random search of online retailers listed in the Winesearcher.com database revealed several that do not charge a significant premium above UPS rates when shipping to the reciprocity states. Thus, it is possible that some online retailers charge more for shipping than our estimates indicate, but this may be offset by the other two factors that tend to inflate our online cost estimates. In any event, the per bottle difference is not very large for six- and 12-bottle orders.

For bricks-and-mortar stores, transportation costs were calculated using the standard government reimbursement for automobile travel ($0.365 per mile), multiplied by the round-trip distance of the store from McLean, Virginia, as indicated by Yahoo! Maps. These costs were divided by the various numbers of bottles (1, 6, or 12) we assumed the customer purchases. Readers might argue that this method also might overstate transportation costs because consumers might combine their shopping trips for wine with other errands. While this concern may be valid, it is our belief that this method might actually *understate* the relative costs associated with driving around Northern Virginia (especially in peak travel times, such as rush hour). It goes without saying that this method for calculating transportation costs does not account for the opportunity costs associated with visiting numerous wine stores and searching for the lowest-priced wines. Research in transportation economics suggests that individuals attach widely varying valuations to travel time, suggesting that opportunity costs of visiting bricks-and-mortar wine stores may vary widely across customers (Small, Winston, and Yan 2002).

These weaknesses aside, calculating travel costs solely based on mileage reimbursement seemed like the most systematic method to determine the additional expense associated with purchases made at local retailers. To the extent that this procedure understates the true expenses associated with transporting wines in Northern Virginia, the reader should take this matter into account when considering the following results.

Using this imputed transportation cost data, we were able to calculate the total price for each bottle on our list, purchased in various quantities.[21] The total price is the sum of the lowest retail price (online or offline) and the relevant transportation cost associated with delivering it to a home residence (via shipping or driving reimbursement). Descriptive statistics for wine prices and transportation costs are presented in Table 1.[22]

Section 4: Findings

The price and availability data do not permit us to make a comprehensive analysis of the effect of the direct shipment ban on consumer welfare. A measurement of overall consumer welfare would require quantity data that are not available, data on factors other than price and variety that consumers value, and data on consumer search patterns. Nor should our calculations be viewed as a "comparative static" analysis of the online and offline market equilibria in the presence and absence of the direct shipping ban. Online prices and variety currently may differ from offline prices and variety, but it is possible that the long-run equilibrium in the absence of the direct shipping ban could involve a different set of prices or different selection as bricks-and-mortar stores alter their prices

---

[21] We ignore quantity discounts, based on our experience that online and offline retailers usually offer similar quantity discounts for purchase of a whole case.
[22] An interesting feature of the data is that the lowest online prices overwhelmingly come not from wineries, but from out-of-state retail outlets that have web-accessible inventories and are listed on winesearcher.com.

and product selection in response to online competition. A comprehensive long-run analysis would need to take any such changes into account.

Nevertheless, our data do help us assess whether the direct shipping ban in the short run prevents consumers from accessing various wines or prices they could not otherwise receive. In that sense, our study is similar to the pre-deregulation studies that compared air fares in unregulated intrastate markets with regulated interstate fares for flights of similar length. (See, e.g., Levine 1965.) Our results should be interpreted as an indicator of the potential for direct shipment to offer price and variety benefits to consumers, rather than a quantitative prediction of the size of these benefits if the direct shipment ban were lifted.

Selection

While we are considering a relatively small product sample in this study, it is instructive to investigate whether consumers' choices are limited because they are not able to shop online for wine from out-of-state vendors. Table 2 lists the wines that were unavailable in Virginia bricks-and-mortar wine retailers within a 10-mile radius of McLean. In total, 15 of the 83 wines in our sample (approximately 18 percent) are unavailable through the Virginia retail outlets searched. In comparison, only 4 of the 83 wines in our sample (approximately 5 percent) could not be found through retail channels online. When excluding from consideration the one wine unavailable online and the three wines that could not be found online or offline, we find that 12 of the 79 wines available online (15 percent) are not available in bricks-and-mortar stores within ten miles of McLean.[23]

---

[23] Three of the four wines that were unavailable online could also not be found in bricks-and-mortar outlets (the exception being Rombauer Vineyards' Napa Valley Chardonnay).

An additional issue emerges when considering the characteristics of some of the bottles that are unavailable in the McLean vicinity. The last column of Table 2 presents the *Wine and Spirits* popularity ranking for each bottle. For the bottles that are unavailable in the McLean vicinity, 8 out of 15 (approximately 53 percent) come from among the 20 most popular bottles, according to *Wine and Spirits'* restaurant poll. This finding may mean that some wineries have neglected to gain state approval for sale of popular labels in Virginia, or that wholesalers or retailers in McLean have neglected to carry some wines that would be popular with the region's consumers, or merely that there are regional differences in demand for various wines.

Clearly, though, the McLean consumers who want to purchase these wines are adversely affected by the direct sales ban. For McLean consumers to acquire these bottles, they would have to either widen their search perimeter beyond the 10-mile radius employed here, request special orders through their local retailers (if such arrangements could be made), or risk breaking the law by having wine shipped directly to their residences by merchants employing 3rd-party shipping agents. Regardless of which avenue they chose, it likely would be less convenient for consumers (from a search cost standpoint) to acquire these bottles through bricks-and-mortar outlets than to use the Internet.

Price

Virginia's ban on out-of-state direct wine shipments might also affect the prices available to consumers. To assess the cost differences between shopping online and offline, Table 3a presents the average cost savings and/or cost penalties from shopping online for the entire sample of 67 wines that could be found in Virginia bricks-and-mortar outlets. Cost differences were calculated first as the difference between the lowest offline price and the lowest online price found via winesearcher.com, or at a given winery's website. We then recalculated cost differences including transportation costs for a variety of shipping options.

The average figures reported in the tables usually reflect a combination of cost savings for online purchase of some wines and cost penalties for online purchase of other wines. Except for the tables reporting results for the most expensive wines, there are always at least a few wines that are cheaper offline, regardless of shipping method. A consumer who purchased each wine from the least expensive source could thus enjoy greater cost savings than our average percentage figures imply.

As is evident from Table 3a, price comparisons between the Internet and bricks-and-mortar stores favor the Internet, where the average price of a bottle in the sample (not accounting for transportation/shipping and handling costs) is $5.84 less if purchased online.[24] The picture changes, however, if one considers shipping expenses, and the lowest-cost option depends on the quantity ordered and shipping method. Depending on the quantity and shipping method, an online customer might save as much as $3.54 per bottle on average when buying a whole case and shipping via ground, or pay as much as $7.26 per bottle more on average if shipping a single bottle via 2nd Day Air. For the most likely quantities – 6 or 12 bottles – the online consumer saves several dollars per bottle if shipping via ground, but the cost difference when shipping via air is not statistically significant.

---

[24] We opted to exclude Virginia's 40 cents/liter excise tax on wine from the analysis, because the size of these price differences makes it clear that the excise tax would not significantly alter the results.

Given that wine is a somewhat perishable product (in the sense that a consumer would not want to expose his bottles to extreme heat or cold) it is likely that many shipments would occur through the faster shipping channels such as 3rd Day or 2nd Day Air, in comparison to standard ground service.[25] Hence, while consumers could obviously acquire some wine cheaper online, the incorporation of transportation costs makes it less clear which channel is dominant for consumers who wish to acquire all of the wines in our sample. Nevertheless, it is worth noting that consumers consistently pay more online only when ordering single bottles.

Another perspective can be gained by considering the cost differences between online and offline sales for the more expensive bottles in the sample. Tables 3b and 3c present the average cost savings from shopping online for wines that have offline retail prices equal to or greater than $20.00 and $40.00, respectively.[26] While the sample size decreases when considering these sub samples, dropping from 67 to 36 for bottles equal to or greater than $20.00, and from 36 to 9 for bottles equal to or greater than $40.00, the potential gains from shopping online increase. For the sample of bottles equal to or greater than $20.00, a McLean consumer has the opportunity to save anywhere from $4.40 to $7.19 per bottle on average by shopping online, depending on the quantity purchased and shipping method employed. (After taking shipping costs into account, only two wines priced at or above $20 are less expensive purchased by the case offline.)

---

[25] The extent to which consumers would prefer to use a faster shipping method will be affected, in large part, by the time of the year that the wine is being purchased. As noted by one California wine retailer with an online presence (www.beltramos.com) if wine needs to be shipped in very cold or very warm weather, they recommend "the fastest service possible."

[26] Transportation costs were recalculated in the appropriate manner to account for consolidation of orders from identical retail outlets.

Cost differences for 2nd Day Air, and for purchase of a single bottle via 3d Day Air, are not significantly different from zero.

Alternatively, for bottles that are equal to or greater than $40.00 in price, a McLean consumer can save an average of between $15.00 and $18.45 per bottle by shopping online rather than offline. All of the wines priced at or above $40 are less expensive by the case when purchased online, regardless of shipping method. As with the "Over $20" sample, cost differences for 2nd Day Air are not significantly different from zero, except for purchase of a whole case. Hence, it seems clear that at least for the more expensive products, consumers could experience significant savings if the ban were lifted.

The fact that removing direct shipment bans would favor those consumers who are in the market for more expensive wines is further supported by considering Table 3d, which presents the cost savings and extra expenses from shopping online for only those bottles that are less expensive than $20.00. While average online prices are $1.66 lower than average offline prices, these savings quickly wash away when incorporating the relevant shipping and handling charges. Depending on the quantity and shipping method, consumers stand to pay an average of between $0.94 and $11.39 more per bottle by shopping online rather than in bricks-and-mortar stores.

Tables 4a, 4b, and 4c present the data from a slightly different perspective, showing the proportional online cost savings. The entire sample of wines online would be 3.6 percent less expensive (on average) than buying them in a store if purchased by the case and shipped via UPS ground service. The average single bottle would be almost 48 percent more expensive if purchased online and shipped via UPS 2nd Day Air, and even a case would be at least 7 percent more expensive if shipped via air. Alternatively, for the wines priced at $20 and above, it would cost an average of 7 percent to 13 percent less (depending on the quantity) to purchase them online and ship via ground service. Savings are negligible or nonexistent if the consumer chooses 2nd or 3d Day Air. Finally, the consumer can save an average of 13 percent to 21 percent on the "$40 and up" wines, depending on the quantity and shipping method. Once again, this result supports the notion that the typical consumer who seeks higher-priced wines could pay less if the direct sales ban were removed.

Table 4d presents the extra cost of buying bottles less than $20.00 online versus offline. While purchasing the lower priced bottles online can save consumers almost 10 percent of what they would pay in bricks-and-mortar stores, this saving evaporates once shipping and handling costs are incorporated into the equation. Consumers would find themselves paying between 8 percent and 83 percent more when purchasing wine online, depending on the quantity and shipping method.

Section 5: Conclusion

While electronic commerce has grown to encompass many business-to-consumer transactions, existing laws and regulations prevent certain industries from carrying out their activities on the Web. Current bans on direct shipment prevent a nationwide virtual wine store from emerging anytime in the near future. This study has discussed the legal framework currently governing alcohol sales and has made a modest attempt to assess whether Virginia's prohibition on interstate direct shipment affects the prices and variety available to Virginia consumers.

Focusing on consumers in McLean, Virginia, and considering a particular search behavior for a bundle of highly popular wines identified by *Wine and Spirits* magazine, our results suggest that McLean consumers may face higher prices and have access to less product variety than they would in the absence of the direct sales ban. Specifically, approximately 15 percent of the wines in our sample are unavailable in 13 bricks-and-mortar stores identified as wine retailers within 10 miles of McLean, but could be ordered online if direct shipment were legal. The effect on consumers may be more significant than this percentage suggests, for two reasons. First, since the sample consists of the more popular wines, it excludes thousands of lesser-known labels that may not be carried by bricks-and-mortar retailers. Second, to the extent that individuals have heterogeneous and strongly-held preferences, the consumers who sought to purchase these wines may be significantly worse off if they settle for less-preferred substitutes.

Many consumers also forego price savings as a result of the ban on direct shipment. On average, consumers could save money on the wines in our sample if they could acquire them from out-of-state vendors, purchase six or 12 bottles, and have them delivered via standard UPS ground service. This finding does not, however, apply to all wines in the sample. For bottles costing less than $20, consumers stand to spend 8 percent to 83 percent more per bottle when shopping online versus shopping offline once transportation charges are taken into account. For wines costing more than $20/bottle, online purchase would save as much as 13 percent on average, depending on the quantity and shipping method. Average savings of up to 21 percent are available on wines costing more than $40/bottle. Many of these averages obscure differences between the costs of individual wines; even for the least expensive shipping method, some individual wines priced below $40 are always less expensive offline.

Similar to the findings on variety, it is important to remember that these results likely understate the potential cost savings that come from shopping online. The method employed for calculating shipping costs from remote vendors was conservative. If wine drinkers obtain economies of scale in shipping by ordering more than one wine at a time from the same online retailer, then the available savings from shopping online are usually larger for the consumer who wants only one or two bottles of a given wine.

It is not clear from the data whether these price savings result from lower search costs, mitigation of market power, or lower costs of online retailers. The price savings are largest for the most expensive wines – precisely the ones more likely to be purchased by wealthy individuals with high search costs or connoisseurs for whom product differentiation would matter most. If online wine retailers succeeded in charging a premium for convenience or for product differentiation, then we would expect to see higher online prices for the more expensive bottles.

In considering these conclusions, a few caveats should be noted. First, it is important to emphasize that these findings are based on a short-run partial equilibrium analysis that does not address how online and offline vendors might alter their prices and product selection if the direct sales ban were lifted. If interstate direct shipment into Virginia were legalized, it is possible that offline retailers would reduce prices or offer access to greater inventory, which would benefit consumers but reduce or eliminate the disparity between online and offline variety and price. It is also conceivable that competition from online retailers might reduce variety available offline if the offline segment of the market contracts significantly. (But see McFadden 2002.) Further research, in the form of some sort of event history analysis, could try to address this issue more completely by comparing changes in prices and product variety before and after a state altered its alcohol sales and importation laws.[27] Studies comparing similar geographic markets in states with different alcohol laws would also help to provide information about the differences in marketing and retail institutions under different legal regimes. Our findings suggest that such studies may well be worth pursuing.

Second, given the small sample size and the limited scope of the geographic market being analyzed, one should be aware of the limits on generalizing from these results. Future research could easily address this issue by replicating this analysis with other geographic markets that are subject to restrictive alcohol sales and importation laws, as well as using a larger sample of wines.

Finally, we should emphasize that our results reflect assumptions about consumer search behavior that we believe are plausible, but different assumptions might lead to different results. For example, if serious wine consumers include grocery stores in their search, then it is possible that they might find some lower offline prices than we found – especially if they time their purchases to coincide with grocery stores' weekly advertised specials. If a McLean wine drinker is unlikely to travel as much as 10 miles to some of the specialty wine shops in Northern Virginia, then average offline prices might be higher or variety lesser than our results indicate.

---

[27] Virginia's governor is currently considering a bill that would legalize interstate direct shipping, and interstate direct shipment bans have also been overturned by courts in North Carolina, New York and Texas. If these states change their policies, their experience could provide data for such analysis.

These caveats aside, this study adds to the debate over the benefits to consumers from legalizing interstate alcohol sales, which would be necessary to facilitate the development of widespread electronic commerce in wine. Further research will only enhance our understanding of the size and scope of the benefits that consumers stand to gain by the development of an additional electronic marketplace.

Table 1: Descriptive Statistics

Variable	Mean	Std. Dev.	Min	Max	Obs.
Lowest Online Price	25.969	20.980	7.970	129.990	79
Lowest Offline Price	28.290	23.916	8.490	169.990	68
Transportation Costs (Buying 1 Bottle)	1.655	2.512	0.073	7.3	68
Transportation Costs per Bottle (Buying 6 Bottles)	0.276	0.419	0.122	1.217	68
Transportation Costs per Bottle (Buying 12 Bottles)	0.138	0.209	0.006	0.608	68
Ground Shipment Costs (Buying 1 Bottle)	5.960	0.583	4.530	6.300	79
3rd Day Air Shipment Costs (Buying 1 Bottle)	9.985	1.714	6.350	10.980	79
2nd Day Air Shipment Costs (Buying 1 Bottle)	13.215	1.943	8.560	14.310	79
Ground Shipment Costs per Bottle (Buying 6 Bottles)	2.834	0.685	1.493	3.248	79
3rd Day Air Shipment Costs per Bottle (Buying 6 Bottles)	5.532	1.294	2.557	6.287	79
2nd Day Air Shipment Costs per Bottle (Buying 6 Bottles)	7.033	1.617	3.232	7.940	79
Ground Shipment Costs per Bottle (Buying 12 Bottles)	2.504	0.711	1.051	2.932	79
3rd Day Air Shipment Costs per Bottle (Buying 12 Bottles)	4.737	1.150	2.072	5.404	79
2nd Day Air Shipment Costs per Bottle (Buying 12 Bottles)	6.115	1.532	2.594	6.982	79

Table 2: Wines Unavailable at Bricks and Mortar Retail Outlets

Winery	Varietal[28]	Wine Label	Bottle Rank
Cakebread Cellars	CA	Napa Valley	16
Caymus Vineyards	CA	Napa Vly. Special Selection	49
Duckhorn Vineyards	M	Three Palms	8
Ferrari-Carano Winery	CH	Alexander Vly. Reserve	7
Ferrari-Carano Winery	M	Alexander Valley	22
Ferrari-Carano Winery	SB	Alexander Valley Fume	40
Jordan Vineyard & Winery	CA	Alexander Valley Estate	24
Kendall-Jackson Vineyards*	CA	Calif. Proprietors Reserve	49
Kendall-Jackson Vineyards*	M	Calif. Proprietors Reserve	15
La Crema (Kendall-Jackson)	P	Russian River Valley	49
Murphy Goode Estate	SB	Fume Reserve	49
Robert Mondavi Winery	CA	Napa Valley	19
Stag's Leap Wine Cellars	CA	SLD Fay	11
Sterling Vineyards*	M	Central Coast – Vintners Collection	6
The Hess Collection	CA	Napa Valley (Mt. Veeder)	9

[28] The abbreviations for varietals are as follows: CH = Chardonnay; CA= Cabernet Sauvignon; SB = Sauvignon Blanc, M = Merlot; P = Pinot Noir; Z = Zinfandel. An asterisk (*) indicates that the bottle could not be found in any Internet inventories.

Table 3a: Cost Savings (Extra Expenses) per Bottle When Shopping Online for Entire Sample[29]

Category	Mean	Std. Dev.	Min.	Max.	Obs.
Online Savings (no transportation costs)	5.838**	10.579	-2.200	83.000	67
Online Savings (UPS Ground Service - Buying 1 Bottle)	1.507	11.560	-8.427	82.686	67
Online Savings (UPS 3rd Day Air - 1 Bottle)	-2.443*	11.518	13.107	78.006	67
Online Savings (UPS 2nd Day Air - 1 Bottle)	-7.256**	10.556	16.510	68.690	67
Online Savings per Bottle (UPS Ground Service - 6 Bottles)	3.342**	10.701	-5.436	80.749	67
Online Savings per Bottle (UPS 3rd Day Air - 6 Bottles)	0.7066	10.720	-8.475	77.711	67
Online Savings per Bottle (UPS 2nd Day Air - 6 Bottles)	-0.767	10.748	-10.128	76.058	67
Online Savings per Bottle (UPS Ground Service - 12 Bottles)	3.543**	10.633	-5.126	80.567	67
Online Savings per Bottle (UPS 3rd Day Air - 12 Bottles)	1.353	10.644	-7.598	78.095	67
Online Savings per Bottle (UPS 2nd Day Air - 12 Bottles)	0.11	10.668	-9.176	76.517	67

Table 3b: Cost Savings (Extra Expenses) per Bottle When Shopping Online for Wines Greater or Equal to $20.00 (Offline Price)

Category	Mean	Std. Dev.	Min.	Max.	Obs.
Online Savings (no transportation costs)	9.435**	13.376	-2.000	83.000	36
Online Savings (UPS Ground Service - 1 Bottle)	5.512**	14.348	-8.008	82.686	36
Online Savings (UPS 3rd Day Air - 1 Bottle)	1.526	14.268	-12.688	78.006	36
Online Savings (UPS 2nd Day Air - 1 Bottle)	-3.693	13.234	-16.310	68.690	36
Online Savings per Bottle (UPS Ground Service - 6 Bottles)	7.027**	13.446	-5.200	80.749	36
Online Savings per Bottle (UPS 3rd Day Air - 6 Bottles)	4.396*	13.432	-8.238	77.711	36
Online Savings per Bottle (UPS 2nd Day Air - 6 Bottles)	2.912	13.45	-9.891	76.058	36
Online Savings per Bottle (UPS Ground Service - 12 Bottles)	7.194**	13.371	-4.907	80.567	36
Online Savings per Bottle (UPS 3rd Day Air - 12 Bottles)	5.005**	13.361	-7.380	78.095	36
Online Savings per Bottle (UPS 2nd Day Air - 12 Bottles)	3.654	13.367	-8.957	76.517	36

---

[29] For Tables 3a, 3b, 3c and 3d, a double asterisk (**) indicates significance greater than the 95% confidence level. A single asterisk (*) indicates significance greater than the 90% confidence level (two-tailed test).

Table 3c: Cost Savings (Extra Expenses) per Bottle When Shopping Online for Wines Greater or Equal to $40.00 (Offline Price)

Category	Mean	Std. Dev.	Min.	Max.	Obs.
Online Savings (no transportation costs)	20.607**	23.817	7.000	83.000	9
Online Savings (UPS Ground Service - 1 Bottle)	17.881*	24.827	2.263	82.686	9
Online Savings (UPS 3rd Day Air - 1 Bottle)	13.573	24.596	-1.678	78.006	9
Online Savings (UPS 2nd Day Air - 1 Bottle)	6.969	23.461	-6.310	68.690	9
Online Savings per Bottle (UPS Ground Service - 6 Bottles)	18.388**	23.804	5.376	80.749	9
Online Savings per Bottle (UPS 3rd Day Air - 6 Bottles)	15.762*	23.683	2.772	77.771	9
Online Savings per Bottle (UPS 2nd Day Air - 6 Bottles)	14.28	23.648	1.119	76.057	9
Online Savings per Bottle (UPS Ground Service - 12 Bottles)	18.448**	23.711	5.677	80.567	9
Online Savings per Bottle (UPS 3rd Day Air - 12 Bottles)	16.262*	23.628	3.204	78.095	9
Online Savings per Bottle (UPS 2nd Day Air - 12 Bottles)	14.990*	23.572	1.627	76.517	9

Table 3d: Cost Savings (Extra Expenses) per Bottle When Shopping Online for Wines Less than $20.00 (Offline Price)

Category	Mean	Std. Dev.	Min.	Max.	Obs.
Online Savings (no transportation costs)	1.661**	2.183	-2.200	6.000	31
Online Savings (UPS Ground Service - 1 Bottle)	-3.144**	3.496	-8.427	6.000	31
Online Savings (UPS 3rd Day Air - 1 Bottle)	-7.053**	3.67	-13.107	1.32	31
Online Savings (UPS 2nd Day Air - 1 Bottle)	-11.393**	2.807	-16.510	-5.580	31
Online Savings per Bottle (UPS Ground Service - 6 Bottles)	-0.934**	2.414	-5.436	3.316	31
Online Savings per Bottle (UPS 3rd Day Air - 6 Bottles)	-3.578**	2.656	-8.475	1.392	31
Online Savings per Bottle (UPS 2nd Day Air - 6 Bottles)	-5.039**	2.824	-10.128	2.455	31
Online Savings per Bottle (UPS Ground Service - 12 Bottles)	-0.697	2.362	-5.126	3.644	31
Online Savings per Bottle (UPS 3rd Day Air - 12 Bottles)	-2.888**	2.532	-7.598	1.948	31
Online Savings per Bottle (UPS 2nd Day Air - 12 Bottles)	-4.220**	2.742	-9.176	1.112	31

Table 4a: Proportional Cost Savings (Extra Expenses) per Bottle When Shopping Online for Entire Sample[30]

Category	Mean	Std. Dev.	Min.	Max.	Obs.
Online Savings (no transportation costs)	0.158**	0.13	-0.187	0.488	67
Online Savings (UPS Ground Service - 1 Bottle)	-0.085**	0.272	-0.753	0.470	67
Online Savings (UPS 3rd Day Air - 1 Bottle)	-0.272**	0.368	-1.270	0.443	67
Online Savings (UPS 2nd Day Air - 1 Bottle)	-0.481**	0.430	-1.645	0.390	67
Online Savings per Bottle (UPS Ground Service - 6 Bottles)	0.024	0.184	-0.500	0.459	67
Online Savings per Bottle (UPS 3rd Day Air - 6 Bottles)	-0.103**	0.251	-0.846	0.442	67
Online Savings per Bottle (UPS 2nd Day Air - 6 Bottles)	-0.181**	0.298	-1.038	0.447	67
Online Savings per Bottle (UPS Ground Service - 12 Bottles)	0.036*	0.176	-0.465	0.458	67
Online Savings per Bottle (UPS 3rd Day Air - 12 Bottles)	-0.070**	0.230	-0.744	0.444	67
Online Savings per Bottle (UPS 2nd Day Air - 12 Bottles)	-0.134**	0.266	-0.922	0.435	67

Table 4b: Proportional Cost Savings (Extra Expenses) per Bottle When Shopping Online for Wines Greater or Equal to $20.00 (Offline Price)

Category	Mean	Std. Dev.	Min.	Max.	Obs.
Online Savings (no transportation costs)	0.211**	0.099	-0.061	0.488	36
Online Savings (UPS Ground Service - 1 Bottle)	0.076**	0.143	-0.241	0.470	36
Online Savings (UPS 3rd Day Air - 1 Bottle)	-0.039	0.174	-0.381	0.443	36
Online Savings (UPS 2nd Day Air - 1 Bottle)	-0.182**	0.185	-0.490	0.390	36
Online Savings per Bottle (UPS Ground Service - 6 Bottles)	0.129**	0.106	-0.156	0.459	36
Online Savings per Bottle (UPS 3rd Day Air - 6 Bottles)	0.052**	0.125	-0.248	0.442	36
Online Savings per Bottle (UPS 2nd Day Air - 6 Bottles)	0.008	0.137	-0.297	0.432	36
Online Savings per Bottle (UPS Ground Service - 12 Bottles)	0.134**	0.104	-0.147	0.458	36
Online Savings per Bottle (UPS 3rd Day Air - 12 Bottles)	0.070**	0.118	-0.222	0.444	36
Online Savings per Bottle (UPS 2nd Day Air - 12 Bottles)	0.031	0.13	-0.269	0.435	36

---

[30] For Tables 4a, 4b, 4c and 4d, a double asterisk (**) indicates significance greater than the 95% confidence level. A single asterisk (*) indicates significance greater than the 90% confidence level (two-tailed test).

Table 4c: Proportional Cost Savings (Extra Expenses) per Bottle When Shopping Online for Wines Greater or Equal to $40.00 (Offline Price)

Category	Mean	Std. Dev.	Min.	Max.	Obs.
Online Savings (no transportation costs)	0.253**	0.122	0.078	0.488	9
Online Savings (UPS Ground Service - 1 Bottle)	0.196**	0.136	0.025	0.470	9
Online Savings (UPS 3rd Day Air - 1 Bottle)	0.129**	0.142	-0.034	0.443	9
Online Savings (UPS 2nd Day Air - 1 Bottle)	0.03	0.147	-0.107	0.390	9
Online Savings per Bottle (UPS Ground Service - 6 Bottles)	0.206**	0.121	0.060	0.459	9
Online Savings per Bottle (UPS 3rd Day Air - 6 Bottles)	0.166**	0.128	0.038	0.442	9
Online Savings per Bottle (UPS 2nd Day Air - 6 Bottles)	0.143**	0.133	0.017	0.432	9
Online Savings per Bottle (UPS Ground Service - 12 Bottles)	0.207**	0.12	0.064	0.458	9
Online Savings per Bottle (UPS 3rd Day Air - 12 Bottles)	0.173**	0.126	0.041	0.444	9
Online Savings per Bottle (UPS 2nd Day Air - 12 Bottles)	0.152**	0.13	0.021	0.435	9

Table 4d: Proportional Cost Savings (Extra Expenses) per Bottle When Shopping Online for Wines Less than $20.00 (Offline Price)

Category	Mean	Std. Dev.	Min.	Max.	Obs.
Online Savings (no transportation costs)	0.097**	0.136	-0.187	0.334	31
Online Savings (UPS Ground Service - 1 Bottle)	-0.272**	0.267	-0.753	0.228	31
Online Savings (UPS 3rd Day Air - 1 Bottle)	-0.543**	0.347	-1.270	0.050	31
Online Savings (UPS 2nd Day Air - 1 Bottle)	-0.828**	0.365	-1.650	-0.278	31
Online Savings per Bottle (UPS Ground Service - 6 Bottles)	-0.097**	0.181	-0.501	0.165	31
Online Savings per Bottle (UPS 3rd Day Air - 6 Bottles)	-0.283**	0.242	-0.843	0.070	31
Online Savings per Bottle (UPS 2nd Day Air - 6 Bottles)	-0.385**	0.277	-1.030	0.012	31
Online Savings per Bottle (UPS Ground Service - 12 Bottles)	-0.078**	0.174	-0.465	0.182	31
Online Savings per Bottle (UPS 3rd Day Air - 12 Bottles)	-0.232**	0.222	-0.744	0.097	31
Online Savings per Bottle (UPS 2nd Day Air - 12 Bottles)	-0.326**	0.257	-0.922	0.056	31

Appendix A: States and Direct Wine Shipment Laws [31]

Reciprocal States

California	Colorado
Hawaii	Idaho
Illinois	Iowa
Minnesota	Missouri
New Mexico	Oregon
Washington	Wisconsin
West Virginia	

Direct Shipments Prohibited (Non-Felony)

Alabama	Arizona
Arkansas	Delaware
Kansas	Maine
Massachusetts	Michigan
Mississippi	New Jersey
New York	Ohio
Oklahoma	Pennsylvania
South Carolina	South Dakota
Texas	Utah
Vermont	Virginia

Direct Shipments Prohibited (Felony)

Florida	Georgia (without permit)
Indiana	Kentucky
Maryland	North Carolina
Tennessee	

Legal Under Certain Circumstances

Alaska	Connecticut
District of Columbia	Georgia (with permit)
Louisiana	Montana
Nebraska	Nevada
New Hampshire	North Dakota
Rhode Island	Wyoming

---

[31] Information current as of July 2002. Source: www.wineinstitute.org.

Appendix B: Wine and Spirits "Top Fifty" Wines

Winery	Varietal[32]	Wine Label
Beaulieu Vineyard	CA	Napa Valley Tapestry
Beaulieu Vineyard	CA	Napa Valley Rutherford
Benziger Family Winery	CH	Carneros
Beringer Vineyards	CA	Knights Valley
Beringer Vineyards	CA	Napa Valley Private Reserve
Beringer Vineyards	CH	Napa Vly. Private Reserve
Beringer Vineyards	CH	Napa Valley
Blackstone Winery	M	California
Blackstone Winery	M	Napa Valley
Cakebread Cellars	CA	Napa Valley
Cakebread Cellars	CH	Napa Valley
Cakebread Cellars	CH	Napa Valley Reserve
Cakebread Cellars	SB	Napa Valley
Cambria Winery & Vineyard	CH	Santa Maria Vly. Katherine's
Caymus Vineyards	CA	Napa Valley
Caymus Vineyards	CA	Napa Vly. Special Selection
Chalk Hill Winery	CH	Chalk Hill
Chateau St. Jean	CH	Sonoma
Chateau St. Jean	CH	Belle Terre
Chateau Ste. Michelle	M	Washington
Chateau Ste. Michelle	M	Canoe Ridge
Clos du Bois	M	Sonoma
Clos du Bois	M	Alexander Valley
Cuvaison Winery	CH	Napa Valley Carneros
De Loach Vineyards	CH	Sonoma OFS
De Loach Vineyards	CH	Russian River Valley
Duckhorn Vineyards	M	Napa Valley
Duckhorn Vineyards	M	Three Palms
Duckhorn Vineyards	SB	Napa Valley
Ferrari-Carano Winery	CH	Alexander Vly. Reserve
Ferrari-Carano Winery	CH	Alexander Valley
Ferrari-Carano Winery	M	Alexander Valley
Ferrari-Carano Winery	SB	Alexander Valley Fume
Franciscan Oakville Estate	M	Napa Oakville Estates
Frog's Leap Winery	SB	Napa Valley
Grgich Hills Cellar	CH	Napa Valley
J. Lohr Winery	CA	Paso Robles 7 Oaks
J. Lohr Winery	CA	Paso Robles Hilltop
Jordan Vineyard & Winery	CA	Alexander Valley Estate
Jordan Vineyard & Winery	CH	Sonoma Cty. Estate
Kendall-Jackson Vineyards	CA	Calif. Vinters Reserve
Kendall-Jackson Vineyards*	CA	Calif. Proprietors Reserve
Kendall-Jackson Vineyards	CH	Calif. Vinters Reserve
Kendall-Jackson Vineyards	CH	Calif. Grand Reserve
Kendall-Jackson Vineyards	M	Calif. Vinters Reserve
Kendall-Jackson Vineyards*	M	Calif. Proprietors Reserve

[32] The abbreviations for varietals are as follows: CH = Chardonnay; CA= Cabernet Sauvignon; SB = Sauvignon Blanc, M − Merlot; P = Pinot Noir; Z = Zinfandel. An asterisk (*) indicates that the bottle could not be found in any Internet inventories.

La Crema (Kendall-Jackson)	P	Russian River Valley
Landmark Vineyards	CH	Sonoma Overlook
Markham Winery	M	Napa Valley
Murphy Goode Estate	SB	Fume
Murphy Goode Estate	SB	Fume Reserve
Ravenswood	Z	Sonoma Vitners Blend
Ravenswood	Z	Lodi
Ridge Vineyards	Z	Lytton Springs
Ridge Vineyards	Z	Geyserville
Robert Mondavi Winery	CA	Napa Valley
Robert Mondavi Winery	CA	North Coast Coastal
Rodney Strong Vineyards	CH	Chalk Hill
Rodney Strong Vineyards	CH	Sonoma
Rodney Strong Vineyards	M	Sonoma
Rombauer Vineyards*	CH	Napa Valley
Rombauer Vineyards	CH	Napa Valley Carneros
Rombauer Vineyards	M	Napa Valley
Rutherford Hill Winery	M	Napa Valley
Shafer Vineyards	M	Napa Valley
Silver Oak Wine Cellars	CA	Alexander Valley
Silver Oak Wine Cellars	CA	Napa Valley
Simi Winery	CH	Alexander Valley
Sonoma-Cutrer Vineyards	CH	Russian River Ranches
Sonoma-Cutrer Vineyards	CH	Les Pierres
Sonoma-Cutrer Vineyards	CH	Cutrer
Stag's Leap Wine Cellars	CA	Napa Valley
Stag's Leap Wine Cellars	CA	SLD Fay
Stag's Leap Winery	CA	Napa Valley
Stag's Leap Winery	M	Napa Valley
Sterling Vineyards	CA	Napa Valley
Sterling Vineyards	CA	Diamond Mountain Ranch
Sterling Vineyards	M	Napa Valley
Sterling Vineyards*	M	Central Coast - Vintners Collection
The Hess Collection	CA	Calif. Hess Select
The Hess Collection	CA	Napa Valley (Mt. Veeder)
The Hess Collection	CH	Calif. Hess Select
The Hess Collection	CH	Napa Valley

Appendix C: Bricks and Mortar Retailers Searched[33]

1.   Total Beverage*
        1451 Chain Bridge Road
        McLean, VA
        703-749-0011
        Mileage: 0.1

2.   Sutton Place Gourmet
        6655 Old Dominion Dr
        McLean, VA
        703-448-3828
        Mileage: 0.2

3.   Cecile's Wine Cellar
        1351 Chain Bridge Road
        McLean, VA
        703-356-6500
        Mileage: 0.4

4.   Arrowine
        4508 Lee Highway
        Arlington, VA
        703-525-0990
        Mileage: 4.0

5.   International Wine and Beverage
        4040 Lee Highway
        Arlington, VA
        703-528-2800
        Mileage: 4.5

6.   Norm's Beer and Wine
        136 Branch Road SE
        Vienna, VA
        703-242-0100
        Mileage: 4.6

7.   Vienna Vintner
        233 Maple Ave E
        Vienna, VA
        703-242-9463
        Mileage: 4.9

8.   Classic Wines

---

[33] An asterisk (*) indicates that the price data was collected from the store's online catalogue.

9912 Georgetown Pike #C
Great Falls, VA
703-759-0430
Mileage: 7.4

9.   Total Beverage Landmark*
6240 Little River Turnpike
Alexandria, VA
703-941-1133
Mileage: 8.2

10.   Botstetter's Wine and Gourmet
3690 King Street #J
Alexandria, VA
703-820-8600
Mileage: 8.5

11.   Fern Street Gourmet
1708 Fern Street
Alexandria, VA
703-931-1234
Mileage: 8.8

12.   Daily Planet Wine and Gourmet*
2004 Mount Vernon Ave
Alexandria, VA
703-549-5051
Mileage: 9.9

13.   Rick's Wine and Gourmet
3117 Duke Street
Alexandria, VA
703-823-4600
Mileage: 10.0

References

Bailey, Joseph P. 1998a. "Electronic Commerce: Prices and Consumer Issues for Three Products: Books, Compact Disks, and Software," *Organization for Economic Cooperation and Development*, OECD/GD(98)4.

_____. 1998b. *Intermediation and Electronic Markets: Aggregation and Pricing in Internet Commerce*. Ph.D. Thesis, Massachusetts Institute of Technology.

Bakos, Yannis. 2001. "The Emerging Landscape for Retail E-Commerce," *Journal of Economic Perspectives* 15:1 (Winter): 69-80.

_____. 1997. "Reducing Buyer Search Costs: Implications for Electronic Marketplaces," *Management Science* 43:12: 1676-92.

Brown, Jeffrey R., and Austan Goolsbee. 2002. "Does the Internet Make Markets More Competitive? Evidence from the Life Insurance Industry," *Journal of Political Economy* 110:3 (June): 481-507.

Brynjolfsson, Erik, and Michael Smith. 2000. "Frictionless Commerce? A Comparison of Internet and Conventional Retailers," *Management Science* (April).

Culbertson, W. Patton, and David Bradford. 1991. "The Price of Beer: Some Evidence from Interstate Comparisons," *International Journal of Industrial Organization* 9:2: 275-89.

Degeratu, Alexandru, Arvind Rangaswamy, and Jianan Wu. 1998. "Consumer Choice Behavior in Online and Regular Stores: The Effects of Brand Name, Price, and Other Search Attributes," paper presented at INFORM conference on Marketing Science and the Internet, Cambridge, MA (March).

Ellison, Glenn, and Sara Fisher Ellison. 2001. "Search, Obfuscation, and Price Elasticities on the Internet," manuscript, MIT (January).

Federal Trade Commission. 2002. "Public Workshop: Possibly Anticompetitive Efforts to Restrict Competition on the Internet" (Oct. 8 Transcript) at http://www.ftc.gov/opp/ecommerce/anticompetitive/021008antitrans.pdf

Genesen, Tracy. 2002. "Coalition for Free Trade Position Summary," presented at Federal Trade Commission Workshop on Possible Anti-Competitive Efforts to Restrict Competition on the Internet (October 8).

Gertner, Robert H., and Robert S. Stillman. 2001. "Vertical Integration and Internet Strategies in the Apparel Industry," *Journal of Industrial Economics* 49:4 (December): 417-40.

Goolsbee, Austan. 2001. "Competition in the Computer Industry: Online versus Retail," *Journal of Industrial Economics* 49:4 (December): 487-99.

_____. 2000. "In a World Without Borders: The Impact of Taxes on Internet Commerce," *Quarterly Journal of Economics* 115:2 (May): 561-76.

_____, and Judith Chevalier. 2002. "Measuring Prices and Price Competition Online: Amazon and Barnes and Noble," National bureau of Economic Research Working paper No. W9085 (July).

Gray, C. Boyden. 2002. "Wine and Spirits Wholesalers of America Summary Position Paper," presented at Federal Trade Commission Workshop on Possible Anti-Competitive Efforts to Restrict Competition on the Internet (October 8).

Gross, Steve. 2002. "Wine Institute Position Summary," presented at Federal Trade Commission Workshop on Possible Anti-Competitive Efforts to Restrict Competition on the Internet (October 8).

Hurd, William H. 2002. "Remarks of William H. Hurd," presented at Federal Trade Commission Workshop on Possible Anti-Competitive Efforts to Restrict Competition on the Internet (October 8).

Jordan, W. John, and Bruce L. Jaffee. 1987. "The Use of Exclusive Territories in the Distribution of Beer: Theoretical and Empirical Observations," *Antitrust Bulletin* 32:1 (Spring): 137-64.

Lee, Ho Geun. 1997. "Do Electronic Marketplaces Lower the Price of Goods?," *Communications of the ACM* 41:12.

Levine, Michael E. (1965) "Is Regulation Necessary?: California Air Transportation and National Regulatory Policy," *Yale Law Journal* 74 (July): 1416-47.

Lynch, John G., and Dan Ariely. 2000. "Wine Online: Search Costs Affect Competition on Price, Quality, and Distribution," *Marketing Science* 19:1 (Winter): 83-103.

McFadden, Daniel L. 2002. "Interstate Wine Shipments and E-Commerce," presented at Federal Trade Commission Workshop on Possible Anti-Competitive Efforts to Restrict Competition on the Internet (October 8).

Mead, Irene M. 2002. "State of Michigan's Remarks," presented at Federal Trade Commission Workshop on Possible Anti-Competitive Efforts to Restrict Competition on the Internet (October 8).

Painter, Murphy J. 2002. "Statement of Murphy J. Painter on Behalf of the Joint Committee of the States," presented at Federal Trade Commission Workshop on Possible Anti-Competitive Efforts to Restrict Competition on the Internet (October 8).

Sass, Tim R., and David S. Saurman. 1996. "Efficiency Effects of Exclusive Territories: Evidence from the Indiana Beer Market," *Economic Inquiry* 34:3 (July): 597-615.

Scott Morton, Fiona, Florian Zettelmeyer and Jorge Silva-Risso. 2001. "Internet Car Retailing," *Journal of Industrial Economics* 49:4 (December): 501-19.
Sloane, David. 2002. "Summary Statement of the American Vintners Association," presented at Federal Trade Commission Workshop on Possible Anti-Competitive Efforts to Restrict Competition on the Internet (October 8).

Small, Kenneth A., Clifford Winston, and Jia Yan. 2002. "Uncovering the Distribution of Motorists' Preferences for Travel Time and Reliability: Implications for Road Pricing," unpublished manuscript, University of California, Irvine.

Smith, Michael D., Joseph Bailey, and Erik Brynjolfsson. 2000. "Understanding Digital Markets: Review and Assessment," in E. Brynjolfsson and B. Kahin, eds. *Understanding the Digital Economy: Data, Tools, and Research.* Cambridge: MIT Press: 99-136

Wine and Spirits, April 2002.

Wiseman, Alan E. 2000. *Economic Perspectives on the Internet.* Washington, DC: Bureau of Economics, Federal Trade Commission.

Zettelmeyer, Florian, Fiona Scott Morton, and Jorge Silva-Risso. 2001. "Cowboys or Cowards? Why are Internet Car Prices Lower?," National Bureau of Economic Research Working Paper No. 86

www.ingramcontent.com/pod-product-compliance
Lightning Source LLC
Chambersburg PA
CBHW081908170526
45167CB00007B/3204